From Ancient Civilizations to Modern Nation

A Comprehensive History of Somalia

Hiba Ali

CONTENTS

Title Page
Book Introduction
Chapter 1: The Prehistoric Era of Somalia   1
Chapter 1: The Rise of Ancient Somali City-States   3
Chapter 2: The Impact of European Colonization   5
Chapter 3: Somali Independence and the Quest for Unity   7
Chapter 4: The Rise of Islamist Extremism   9
Chapter 5: The Humanitarian Crisis in Somalia   11
Chapter 6: Countering Extremism in Somalia   13
Chapter 7: Prospects for the Future   15
Chapter 8: Conclusion   17
Chapter 9: Recommendations   18
Chapter 10: The Role of International Community   20
Chapter 11: The Future of Somalia   22
Chapter 12: Conclusion   24
Chapter 13: Recommendations   26
Chapter 14: Conclusion   28
Epilogue   29

BOOK INTRODUCTION

Somalia, located in the Horn of Africa, has a rich and diverse history that dates back to prehistoric times. The country has witnessed the rise and fall of ancient city-states, the emergence of powerful sultanates, and the colonization by various foreign powers. In modern times, Somalia has undergone a series of political upheavals, including a military dictatorship, a civil war, and the rise of terrorist groups.

This book aims to provide a comprehensive overview of Somali history, from the prehistoric era to the present day. It will explore the key events and developments that have shaped the Somali people and their culture, as well as the political and economic forces that have influenced the country's trajectory.

The book is organized into fifteen chapters, each of which covers a specific period or topic in Somali history. The first chapter explores the prehistoric era of Somalia, including the early human settlements and the development of agriculture. Subsequent chapters examine the rise and fall of ancient Somali city-states, the emergence of powerful sultanates, and the impact of foreign invasions and colonization. Later chapters delve into modern Somali history, including the struggle for independence, the rise of military dictatorship, and the civil war that followed. The book also examines the role of various actors in Somali politics, including warlords, foreign powers, and international organizations. Finally, the book concludes with an analysis of the challenges and opportunities facing Somalia today.

CHAPTER 1: THE PREHISTORIC ERA OF SOMALIA

The prehistoric era of Somalia, also known as the Stone Age, spans from around 2.6 million years ago to the advent of agriculture around 5,000 years ago. During this period, early humans lived in the area and developed various hunting and gathering techniques to survive in the harsh environment.

One of the most significant discoveries of the prehistoric era in Somalia was the Laas Geel rock paintings, which were discovered in 2002. These paintings, estimated to be around 9,000 years old, depict scenes of hunting, herding, and dancing, as well as images of animals and human figures.

Another notable aspect of the prehistoric era in Somalia was the development of early human tools and technologies. Stone tools such as hand axes, cleavers, and scrapers have been found in various parts of Somalia, indicating the sophistication of early human societies in the region.

In addition to the development of tools and technologies, the prehistoric era of Somalia also saw the emergence of early human settlements. The most famous of these settlements is the site of Hargeisa, which dates back to around 4,000 BCE. Excavations at Hargeisa have revealed evidence of early human structures, including circular huts made from stone and mud.

Overall, the prehistoric era of Somalia provides important insights into the early human history of the region. The development of tools, technologies, and settlements laid the foundation for the later cultural and political developments in Somalia.

However, due to the lack of written records from this time period, much of what we know about prehistoric Somalia is based on archaeological evidence and scientific analysis. As such, there is still much that remains unknown about the early history of Somalia and the lives of its ancient inhabitants.

Despite these challenges, scholars continue to explore the prehistoric era of Somalia and uncover new insights into this important period of human history. Through ongoing excavations, research, and scientific analysis, we can gain a better understanding of the roots of Somali culture and society.

In the following chapters, we will explore the rise and fall of ancient Somali city-states, the emergence of powerful sultanates, and the impact of foreign invasions and colonization. We will also delve into modern Somali history, including the struggle for independence, the rise of military dictatorship, and the civil war that followed. The book will examine the role of various actors in Somali politics, including warlords, foreign powers, and international organizations. Finally, the book will conclude with an analysis of the challenges and opportunities facing Somalia today.

CHAPTER 1: THE RISE OF ANCIENT SOMALI CITY-STATES

The first recorded history of Somalia dates back to the 1st century CE when the ancient Greeks and Romans described a land of trading ports on the East African coast. These ports were part of the network of Indian Ocean trade that connected Africa, Arabia, India, and Southeast Asia.

As the demand for ivory, gold, and spices grew in the Mediterranean world, these trading ports flourished and became the foundation of the first Somali city-states. By the 7th century, several city-states had emerged along the Somali coast, including Mogadishu, Barawa, and Merca.

These city-states were known for their bustling ports, trade in luxury goods, and flourishing urban centers. They were ruled by powerful merchants and elite families who controlled the economy, politics, and culture of their respective regions. The city-states were also home to diverse communities of people, including Arabs, Persians, Indians, and Africans, who intermarried and shared cultural and religious traditions.

However, the rise of Islam in the Arabian Peninsula in the 7th century had a profound impact on Somalia. Arab traders and missionaries spread the Islamic faith to the Somali coast, and many Somalis converted to Islam. This new religion brought with it new political and social structures, as well as a shared sense of identity among Somali Muslims.

As the city-states became more powerful and wealthy, they also became targets of foreign invasions. In the 16th century, the Portuguese attempted to conquer the Somali coast, but were repelled by the powerful Somali sultanates of Ajuran and Adal. These sultanates were known for their military prowess and their resistance to foreign aggression.

Despite these challenges, the city-states continued to thrive, and by the 19th century, they had become important centers of trade and commerce. However, the arrival of European colonial powers in the late 19th century would mark the beginning of a new era in Somali history.

CHAPTER 2: THE IMPACT OF EUROPEAN COLONIZATION

In the late 19th century, European powers began to carve up Africa into colonies. Somalia was no exception, and in 1884, the region was divided into territories controlled by Italy, Britain, and France.

The Italian colony of Somalia was the largest and most significant, encompassing much of southern Somalia and the capital city of Mogadishu. The Italians established a colonial administration and invested in infrastructure and development projects, including the construction of roads, schools, and hospitals.

However, Italian colonial rule was marked by harsh repression and exploitation. The Somalis were subjected to forced labor, taxation, and land confiscation, and their cultural and political institutions were systematically dismantled. Resistance to Italian colonial rule was met with brutal violence, including massacres and torture.

The British and French colonies in Somalia were smaller and less significant, but they too had a profound impact on Somali society. The British established a protectorate in the north of Somalia, while the French controlled the neighboring region of Djibouti. These territories were used as bases for European trade and colonial expansion, and they too were marked by violence and exploitation.

The impact of European colonization on Somalia was devastating, and it would have long-lasting effects on the region. The fragmentation of Somali society, the destruction of cultural and political institutions, and the legacy of violence and exploitation would all contribute to the challenges facing modern Somalia. In the following chapters, we will explore how these legacies have shaped Somali history and society, and the ongoing efforts to overcome them.

CHAPTER 3: SOMALI INDEPENDENCE AND THE QUEST FOR UNITY

After World War II, the tide of decolonization swept across Africa, and Somalia emerged as a major battleground in the struggle for independence. In 1960, Somalia gained its independence from Italy and Britain and became a unified, independent nation.

However, the path to unity and stability would prove to be difficult. Somali society was deeply divided along clan and regional lines, and there was a lack of consensus on how to build a new, unified nation. The new government, led by President Aden Abdullah Osman, faced the daunting task of building a functional state from scratch, and it struggled to balance the interests of the different clans and regions.

Despite these challenges, the early years of independence were marked by significant progress. The government invested in education, health care, and infrastructure, and the country enjoyed a period of relative stability and economic growth. However, this period of progress would be short-lived.

In the late 1960s, a military coup overthrew the civilian government, and Somalia entered a period of authoritarian rule. The new government, led by President Siad Barre, pursued a policy of centralization and state control, which alienated many Somalis and led to increased tensions between the government and the clans.

By the 1980s, Somalia had become increasingly unstable, with a weak central government and a growing insurgency led by clan-based militias. In 1991, the government collapsed, and Somalia descended into a period of civil war and chaos.

The quest for unity and stability remains a central challenge facing Somalia today. Despite the setbacks of the past, there are ongoing efforts to build a more inclusive and representative government, and to address the underlying social and economic inequalities that have contributed to Somalia's instability. In the following chapters, we will explore these efforts in more detail and examine the prospects for a more peaceful and prosperous future for Somalia.

CHAPTER 4: THE RISE OF ISLAMIST EXTREMISM

The collapse of the Somali government in 1991 created a power vacuum that was quickly filled by clan-based militias and warlords. In this chaotic environment, radical Islamist groups emerged, seeking to establish their own brand of order and authority.

One of the most significant of these groups was Al-Shabaab, which emerged in the early 2000s as an offshoot of the Islamic Courts Union (ICU). The ICU had briefly held power in southern Somalia in 2006, before being driven out by a joint Ethiopian-Somali government offensive.

Al-Shabaab filled the void left by the ICU, and quickly established itself as one of the most powerful and ruthless groups in Somalia. It pursued a campaign of terror and violence, targeting government officials, civilians, and aid workers, and imposing a harsh form of Islamic law in areas under its control.

Al-Shabaab's rise to prominence was fueled by a combination of factors, including widespread disillusionment with the weak and corrupt Somali government, a lack of economic opportunities, and the group's ability to provide basic services in areas neglected by the government.

The group's influence reached its peak in 2011, when it controlled large parts of southern Somalia, including the port city of Kismayo. However, a joint offensive by African Union (AU) and Somali government forces eventually drove Al-Shabaab out of these areas, and the group has since been weakened, but not defeated.

The rise of Al-Shabaab has had a profound impact on Somalia, contributing to the country's ongoing instability and posing a threat to regional security. Despite the group's weakening, the underlying factors that fueled its rise remain, and there are concerns that new extremist groups could emerge in the future. In the following chapters, we will explore the impact of extremism on Somalia, and the efforts to counter it.

CHAPTER 5: THE HUMANITARIAN CRISIS IN SOMALIA

Somalia has been plagued by a humanitarian crisis for decades, with millions of people facing extreme poverty, food insecurity, and displacement. The ongoing conflict, natural disasters such as droughts and floods, and the COVID-19 pandemic have all contributed to the worsening of the situation.

The crisis has led to the displacement of millions of people, both within Somalia and in neighboring countries. Many Somalis have been forced to flee their homes multiple times, and the lack of security and basic services has made it difficult for them to rebuild their lives.

In addition, Somalia has one of the highest rates of malnutrition in the world, with almost half of all children under the age of five suffering from stunted growth. Access to health care is limited, and preventable diseases such as malaria and cholera are common.

The humanitarian crisis has been exacerbated by the limited capacity of the Somali government to respond, due to a lack of resources and the ongoing conflict. International aid organizations have played a crucial role in providing lifesaving assistance, but their efforts have been hampered by insecurity and logistical challenges.

Despite these challenges, there are ongoing efforts to address the humanitarian crisis in Somalia. The Somali government and international partners are working to improve access to basic services, such as health care and education, and to build the resilience of communities facing frequent shocks and disasters.

In addition, there is a growing recognition of the need to address the underlying causes of the crisis, such as poverty, inequality, and insecurity. By addressing these root causes, it is hoped that Somalia can achieve long-term stability and prosperity, and break the cycle of humanitarian crisis and conflict.

CHAPTER 6: COUNTERING EXTREMISM IN SOMALIA

The threat of extremism in Somalia has been a major concern for the international community, and efforts to counter it have been ongoing for years. However, progress has been slow, and the threat remains significant.

One approach to countering extremism has been to strengthen the capacity of the Somali government and security forces to provide security and stability. The African Union Mission in Somalia (AMISOM) has played a crucial role in this effort, providing training, equipment, and support to Somali security forces.

In addition, there have been efforts to address the root causes of extremism, such as poverty, unemployment, and marginalization. Programs aimed at providing economic opportunities, education, and social services to vulnerable communities have been implemented by the Somali government and international partners.

Another approach has been to engage with moderate Islamic leaders and scholars, and to promote a message of tolerance and peaceful coexistence. This has included efforts to counter extremist propaganda and to promote alternative narratives through social media and other channels.

Despite these efforts, the threat of extremism remains significant in Somalia, and new groups and ideologies continue to emerge. There are concerns that the ongoing conflict and humanitarian crisis in Somalia provide fertile ground for extremist recruitment and radicalization.

Moving forward, it will be important to continue to strengthen the capacity of the Somali government and security forces, to address the root causes of extremism, and to engage with communities and religious leaders in the fight against extremism. Only through a sustained and coordinated effort can the threat of extremism be effectively countered in Somalia.

CHAPTER 7: PROSPECTS FOR THE FUTURE

Despite the ongoing challenges facing Somalia, there are reasons to be optimistic about the country's future. In recent years, there has been some progress in areas such as security, governance, and economic development.

The Somali government, with the support of the international community, has made significant strides in improving security and governance. The formation of a federal government in 2012 marked a major milestone in Somalia's political transition, and there have been efforts to strengthen institutions and promote transparency and accountability.

In addition, the Somali economy has shown signs of growth and diversification, with sectors such as telecommunications and finance experiencing significant expansion. There is also potential for growth in areas such as agriculture, fisheries, and tourism.

However, much remains to be done to sustain and build on this progress. The ongoing conflict and insecurity in parts of the country continue to hamper development efforts, and the humanitarian crisis remains a major concern.

To realize the full potential of Somalia, it will be important to address the root causes of conflict and instability, including poverty, inequality, and marginalization. This will require a sustained and comprehensive approach, encompassing efforts to promote economic development, strengthen governance and institutions, and address the needs of vulnerable communities.

In addition, there is a need for continued support and engagement from the international community. This includes providing financial and technical assistance, supporting peacekeeping and stabilization efforts, and engaging in dialogue and cooperation with the Somali government and civil society.

While there are significant challenges facing Somalia, there are also opportunities for progress and development. With sustained effort and commitment, it is possible to build a more peaceful, prosperous, and stable Somalia for all its people.

CHAPTER 8: CONCLUSION

Somalia has faced significant challenges over the past few decades, including conflict, insecurity, poverty, and a humanitarian crisis. Despite these challenges, there have been some signs of progress in recent years, particularly in the areas of security, governance, and economic development.

To build on this progress and address the root causes of conflict and instability, it will be important to take a comprehensive and sustained approach. This approach should encompass efforts to promote economic development, strengthen governance and institutions, and address the needs of vulnerable communities.

In addition, there is a need for continued engagement and support from the international community. This includes providing financial and technical assistance, supporting peacekeeping and stabilization efforts, and engaging in dialogue and cooperation with the Somali government and civil society.

Ultimately, the future of Somalia will depend on the ability of its people, institutions, and international partners to work together in pursuit of a common goal: a more peaceful, prosperous, and stable Somalia for all its citizens. While significant challenges remain, there are also opportunities for progress and development, and with sustained effort and commitment, it is possible to build a brighter future for Somalia.

CHAPTER 9: RECOMMENDATIONS

Based on the analysis of Somalia's history and current situation, as well as the prospects for the future, the following recommendations are proposed:

1. Prioritize peacebuilding and conflict resolution efforts: The ongoing conflict and insecurity in Somalia is a major impediment to development and must be addressed. Efforts should be made to promote peacebuilding and conflict resolution through dialogue, negotiation, and reconciliation.

2. Foster economic development and diversification: The Somali economy has significant potential for growth and diversification, particularly in sectors such as agriculture, fisheries, and tourism. Efforts should be made to promote economic development through targeted investments, policy reforms, and improved infrastructure.

3. Strengthen governance and institutions: Strong and effective institutions are essential for sustainable development and stability in Somalia. Efforts should be made to strengthen governance and institutions at all levels, including through reforms to the legal and regulatory framework and the promotion of transparency and accountability.

4. Address the humanitarian crisis: The humanitarian crisis in Somalia is a major concern and requires

sustained attention and support. Efforts should be made to provide humanitarian assistance, improve access to basic services, and promote the rights and well-being of vulnerable communities.

5. Promote regional and international cooperation: Somalia's challenges are not limited to its borders, and regional and international cooperation is essential for addressing them. Efforts should be made to promote dialogue and cooperation with neighboring countries, regional organizations, and international partners, including through the United Nations and other multilateral organizations.

By pursuing these recommendations, it is possible to make significant progress in addressing the challenges facing Somalia and building a more peaceful, prosperous, and stable future for all its citizens.

CHAPTER 10: THE ROLE OF INTERNATIONAL COMMUNITY

The international community has played a significant role in Somalia's history and current situation, and will continue to do so in the future. The role of the international community has been both positive and negative, and has included a range of actors and initiatives.

One of the most significant roles of the international community in Somalia has been providing humanitarian assistance. Somalia has faced numerous humanitarian crises over the past few decades, including droughts, famines, and displacement. International organizations such as the United Nations, non-governmental organizations (NGOs), and donor countries have provided crucial assistance in response to these crises, including food aid, health care, and shelter.

The international community has also played a role in promoting peace and stability in Somalia, through peacekeeping and stabilization efforts. The African Union Mission in Somalia (AMISOM) has been a key actor in this regard, with the support of the United Nations and other partners. While AMISOM has made significant progress in reducing violence and stabilizing some parts of the country, it has also faced criticism and challenges, including allegations of human rights abuses and the withdrawal of some troop-contributing countries.

In addition to these efforts, the international community has also provided financial and technical assistance to support economic development, governance, and institution-building in Somalia.

Donor countries and multilateral organizations such as the World Bank and International Monetary Fund have provided significant support in this regard, including debt relief, development aid, and technical assistance.

However, the role of the international community in Somalia has not been without controversy and criticism. Some have accused external actors of interfering in Somali affairs and imposing their own agendas, while others have raised concerns about the effectiveness and impact of international assistance. Moreover, the international community has at times been accused of failing to adequately consider the needs and perspectives of Somali actors, including civil society and marginalized communities.

In light of these challenges, it is important for the international community to continue to engage with Somalia in a way that is respectful, collaborative, and effective. This includes supporting Somali-led initiatives, promoting local ownership and participation, and taking a long-term and comprehensive approach to development and peacebuilding efforts. Ultimately, the success of international engagement in Somalia will depend on the ability of external actors to work in partnership with Somali actors and support their aspirations for a more peaceful, prosperous, and stable future.

CHAPTER 11: THE FUTURE OF SOMALIA

The future of Somalia remains uncertain, as the country continues to face significant challenges and obstacles. However, there are also opportunities for positive change and progress, particularly if the Somali government and its partners are able to address key issues and capitalize on potential opportunities.

One of the most pressing challenges facing Somalia is security. Despite the progress made by AMISOM and the Somali National Army in reducing violence and combating terrorism, the country remains at risk of attacks from Al-Shabaab and other armed groups. Addressing this challenge will require sustained investment in security sector reform, including efforts to professionalize the Somali security forces, improve coordination and intelligence sharing, and address root causes of conflict.

Another key challenge facing Somalia is economic development. While the country has made progress in recent years, particularly in terms of private sector growth and foreign investment, much more needs to be done to create jobs, address poverty, and reduce inequality. This will require continued efforts to improve infrastructure, expand access to finance and markets, and promote economic diversification and value addition.

Governance and institution-building also remain critical areas of focus for Somalia's future. While the Somali government has made progress in recent years, particularly in terms of constitutional reform and electoral processes, there is still much work to be done to strengthen the rule of law, combat corruption, and improve service delivery. This will require sustained efforts to build institutional capacity, promote accountability, and engage in constructive dialogue with civil society and other stakeholders.

At the same time, there are also opportunities for positive change and progress in Somalia. The country has a young and dynamic population, with significant potential for entrepreneurship, innovation, and social change. Moreover, there are significant natural resources, including fisheries, minerals, and potentially oil and gas, that could provide a foundation for economic growth and development.

Ultimately, the future of Somalia will depend on the ability of the Somali government and its partners to address key challenges and capitalize on potential opportunities. This will require sustained investment, commitment, and collaboration, as well as a long-term and comprehensive approach to development and peacebuilding. By working together, Somalia and its partners can build a more peaceful, prosperous, and stable future for all Somalis.

CHAPTER 12: CONCLUSION

Somalia has a rich and complex history, marked by periods of great prosperity, cultural achievement, and political power, as well as periods of conflict, instability, and external intervention. From the ancient civilization of the Land of Punt, to the powerful Somali sultanates, to the struggles of the colonial and post-colonial eras, Somalia has experienced a wide range of challenges and triumphs.

Today, Somalia faces significant challenges, including ongoing violence and insecurity, economic underdevelopment, and governance and institutional weaknesses. However, there are also opportunities for positive change and progress, particularly if the Somali government and its partners are able to address key issues and capitalize on potential opportunities.

To achieve this, Somalia will need sustained investment, commitment, and collaboration from its partners, including the international community, neighboring countries, and the Somali diaspora. It will also require a long-term and comprehensive approach to development and peacebuilding, grounded in the principles of inclusivity, transparency, and accountability.

Ultimately, the success of Somalia's future will depend on the ability of its people and leaders to come together, transcend their differences, and work towards a shared vision of peace, prosperity, and stability. By building on the strengths of its past, and working together towards a brighter future, Somalia can overcome its challenges and build a more peaceful, prosperous, and stable society for all Somalis.

CHAPTER 13: RECOMMENDATIONS

Based on the history and analysis presented in this book, there are several recommendations for how Somalia can move forward and address the challenges it faces. These recommendations are not exhaustive, and should be considered as a starting point for further discussion and action.

1. Strengthen governance and institutions: Somalia needs to strengthen its governance and institutional framework, including building an effective civil service, judiciary, and security sector. This will require sustained investment in capacity-building, as well as efforts to promote transparency, accountability, and inclusivity.

2. Address root causes of conflict: To address the root causes of conflict in Somalia, it is necessary to address issues of inequality, marginalization, and exclusion. This includes promoting inclusive politics and governance, supporting economic development and job creation, and investing in education and social services.

3. Promote regional cooperation: Somalia's stability and development are closely linked to regional dynamics, and it is therefore important to promote greater regional cooperation and integration. This includes working with neighboring countries to address cross-border security threats, promote economic integration, and facilitate the movement of people and goods.

4. Empower local communities: Local communities in

Somalia have a critical role to play in promoting peace, stability, and development. To empower these communities, it is necessary to promote community-led development, support local governance structures, and invest in basic infrastructure and services.

5. Engage the diaspora: The Somali diaspora represents a significant resource for the country, in terms of financial resources, skills, and expertise. To fully harness this potential, it is necessary to engage the diaspora in a meaningful way, including through the creation of investment and business opportunities, and the promotion of diaspora-led development initiatives.

By implementing these recommendations, Somalia can build a stronger, more stable, and more prosperous society for its people. However, achieving this will require sustained commitment, investment, and collaboration from all stakeholders, including the government, civil society, the private sector, and international partners. With the right approach and a shared vision for the future, Somalia can overcome its challenges and realize its full potential as a peaceful and prosperous nation.

CHAPTER 14: CONCLUSION

Somalia's history is a complex and fascinating one, marked by centuries of trade, empire-building, and cultural exchange, as well as decades of conflict, instability, and humanitarian crises. From the rise of the Somali city-states to the legacy of colonialism, from the civil war to the emergence of a new political order, this book has explored the many twists and turns of Somalia's journey through time.

As we have seen, Somalia's challenges are many and diverse, ranging from political instability and insecurity to economic underdevelopment and social inequality. At the same time, Somalia also has immense potential, including a young and dynamic population, abundant natural resources, and a strategic location at the crossroads of Africa, the Middle East, and Asia.

To realize this potential and overcome its challenges, Somalia will need to draw on its strengths and address its weaknesses, working collaboratively with all stakeholders to build a peaceful, stable, and prosperous society for its people. This will require a sustained and long-term commitment from all actors, including the government, civil society, the private sector, and international partners.

It is my hope that this book has contributed to a better understanding of Somalia's rich history and complex present, and that it has provided a foundation for further study and engagement with this important country. May Somalia continue to strive towards a brighter future for all its citizens.

EPILOGUE

Since the publication of this book, Somalia has continued to face both challenges and opportunities. In recent years, the country has made some progress in stabilizing its political situation, including holding successful presidential and parliamentary elections in 2021, the first such elections in over 50 years. The new government faces many daunting tasks, including addressing security concerns, improving governance, and promoting economic growth and development.

At the same time, Somalia continues to grapple with numerous challenges, including a persistent insurgency by the al-Shabaab militant group, recurring droughts and famines, and the ongoing COVID-19 pandemic. The humanitarian situation in many parts of the country remains dire, with millions of people in need of assistance.

Despite these challenges, there are also many reasons for hope. Somalia's young and educated population, combined with its rich natural resources and strategic location, offer tremendous potential for growth and development. The country has a vibrant private sector and a dynamic civil society, both of which are essential for promoting inclusive economic growth and political stability. Moving forward, it will be critical for all stakeholders to work together in a spirit of cooperation and collaboration to overcome Somalia's challenges and seize its opportunities. This will require sustained and long-term investments in the country's institutions, infrastructure, and human capital, as well as a commitment to promoting peace, security, and respect for human rights.

Ultimately, the future of Somalia will depend on the actions of its people and their leaders, as well as on the support of the international community. As Somalia continues on its journey, let us all hope for a brighter, more peaceful, and prosperous future for this important country and its people.

Printed in Great Britain
by Amazon